HOW TO LIVE THE

VOLUME 1:

A Journal for Finding Peace, Progress and Prosperity in Your Purpose in 21 Days

JENÉ ELAINE WALKER, ED.D.

HOW TO LIVE THE GOLDEN LIFE

VOLUME 1

To God the Father, God the Son Yeshua (Jesus Christ), and God the Holy Spirit, You are the head of my life. I am totally surrendered to You. My life's goal is to please you in my work for the kingdom. May men see everything I do and glorify You.

To my son posthumously John Jaylen Walker Kinnitt, who shared me unselfishly with the world. You are my heart. I miss you so much. I love you with all that I am, and I live for God and you. Even in spirit, you inspire me.

To my mom and dad, Helen and James, thanks for loving me unconditionally. I love you two. To my family, Auntie Forrestine McPherson and Bishop R.R. and Pastor Sharon McPherson, thanks for loving me and praying for me.

To my spiritual parents, Apostle Jonathan and Prophetess Amanda Ferguson. Dad, you told me I am an overcomer and I'm walking in that. I'm living it out right now. And mom, you asked me a hard question, "Do you want to be in the same position this time next year?" You nurtured me back to me. You encourage me to be better.

To women leaders across the nations, I want to coach you until you establish a mental environment for peace, progress, and prosperity to live the golden life you deserve.

CONTENTS

A PERSONAL WORD FROM JENÉ WALKER

I am elated that you have decided that you absolutely cannot settle for another season of mediocrity. You didn't stumble across this journal by happenstance. You are at a crossroads. Either you are going to live the life that is yours by birthright or you will settle into a life of comfortability. I believe that since you've invested in your leadership by purchasing this journal that you're a woman who is serious about taking back everything that belongs to her. How To Live the Golden Life is not for faint hearted women. This journal is more than just a journal but it is a resource for a 21-day spiritual journey. When you do the work, it will build capacity for you to take meaningful and consistent action to live your best life now. Completing this journal can literally prepare your mental environment for a life and leadership of peace, progress and prosperity. So many women leaders haven't realized their ultimate level of kingdom success because they don't know what their purpose is or how to manifest it. Are you a woman who desires to have peace in playing big? Do you need the "ok" or a little bit of coaching to go ahead and make unprecedented progress? Do you need permission to go ahead and seize the millions that belong to you? If your answer is yes to either of these questions then this journal is for you.

This journal is not for the woman who hasn't reached a point of tension or frustration about where she currently is. It's not for the woman leader who is satisfied with her level of leadership and financial status. This journal is for the woman who is ready to be unleashed to be legendary. Is this you? You're a woman leader who is ready to take control of her life – finally. You're ready to be disciplined in order for true transformation to take place in your life and your leadership. You're ready to live your life like it's golden.

I hid, played small, denied myself, and lied to myself for so long. I didn't really believe that there was a higher calling and purpose for my life. And, when I did finally realize it, I was terrified of moving forward in my purpose. Can you relate to this? I've seen so many women invest in coaching and programs for business coaches, financial coaches, book publishing and other strategists and not be able to execute or move forward in any of those strategies or ventures because they don't invest in a mindset coach like me until it is the last resort. But not you, you're here because you know that the golden life is designed for you. You know that your mindset has to be transformed to live the golden life.

You are now about to take strategic actions to transform your mindset so you can fulfill your purpose at your greatest capacity. But first you must throw out and destroy every hindering thought, avoidance behavior, and limiting beliefs that are literally blocking your peace, progress and prosperity (2 Corinthians 10:3-5). Ponder your "why" and your reason for wanting the golden life. Then throw out any misconception of time or the idea that you're running out of it. Then, be willing to commit to daily actions that will ultimately lead to your prospering in your purpose. You will be amazed at how much your mindset has changed at the end of these twenty-one days and I can't wait to hear your testimonies.

Why the How To Live the Golden Life 21-Day Challenge?
I did minimal research on the golden age so I don't know enough about it to compare it to the life God showed me for us after we complete these twenty-one days. Your next twenty-one days can be life changing if you're willing to set aside about one hour each day to dedicate time to your spiritual development and to transforming your mindset. This journal was created to challenge women leaders to begin to live in a perpetual state of "winning." The purpose of this journal is to help women leaders to establish a mental environment for peace, progress, and prosperity. You are about to enter into a season of the golden life. The evidence that you've entered in will be: 1) a season of accomplishing greater tasks; 2) a season of greater clarity about your life purpose; 3) a season of higher levels of achievement; and 4) a season of uncommon spiritual wealth and material prosperity.

Your Next 21 Days
For each day of the twenty-one-day challenge, you will be provided with a **Strategy**, which is the title of the Day. These strategies are overarching actions for you to be able to achieve your peace, make progress, and seize your prosperity. The **Scripture** is the foundation you will need to execute the strategy. Reading, reflecting and meditating on, and studying the scripture for the day will help you manifest the strategy. Then, the **About** each day is a brief commentary on the day's scripture. The **Affirmation** is for you to speak aloud over yourself throughout the day. You may possibly write each affirmation on an index card and keep them on a key ring that

you carry in your purse. The **Take Action** section includes long term actions that you can take to continually live your life like it's golden. The **Thoughts for Your Journal** are a few questions for you to respond to when you write in your journal.

The **Prayer Points** is for you to pray and reflect on. Then, **Your Prayer Points** are for other points you desire to pray each day. **Prayer Strategy** is for you to write the strategy God gives you in prayer. **Other Reference Scriptures** is for you to research and find then write additional scriptures you believe would augment the day's challenge. **Unleashed to Lead** is an opportunity for you to apply what you've read and reflected upon to your leadership role. Then, you will reflect on the type of impact your day had on you. **Impact** is for you to reflect on how the challenge for the day impacted your peace, progress or prosperity. Then, a **Quote of the Day** is included to transform your mindset and inspire you. It is for you to read and ponder its significance in your day. At the end of a seven-day cycle within the twenty-one days, you will have an opportunity to **Review** the topic of the week. There are a few sections that are only in strategic places during the twenty-one days. **The Leadership Profile** is for you to reflect on your characteristics as a leader and how you grow throughout the challenge. **Demonstrate** is for you to take immediate action toward taking back your peace, progress, and prosperity. **Extending the Strategy** is for you to take the challenge and application a step further. **Getting the Picture** incorporates an opportunity for you to create a visual representation of the strategy. **Manifestation** is what you've actually caused to happen for yourself during the challenge.

Make sure you complete your journal sequentially as each strategy builds upon the previous strategies. Only complete one day at a time; however, I recommend that you complete the journal within the twenty-one days to develop a habit of taking consistent action towards your purpose. Finally, it is imperative that you thoughtfully answer all questions and complete every activity in order to transform your mindset to live the golden lifestyle you desire.

YOUR TWENTY-ONE DAYS BEGIN TODAY

Commitment Statement:

I commit to taking daily strategic action from _____
to _____ to ultimately manifest my peace, progress, and
prosperity.

I am committing to these twenty-one days because I want to

_____

I am willing to make the following changes to my daily routine
to accommodate my journey:

_____

I am anticipating the following results at the end of the
twenty-one days:

HAVING *Peace* IN PURSUING YOUR *Purpose*

Day 1: UNDERSTAND GOD'S GREATER PURPOSE FOR MANKIND

Genesis 1:26 (AMPC) "God said, Let Us Father, Son, and Holy Spirit] make mankind in Our image, after Our likeness, and let them have complete authority over the fish of the sea, the birds of the air, the tame beasts, and over all of the earth, and over everything that creeps upon the earth."

ABOUT DAY 1

One common crisis among women leaders is not truly understanding why we were put on this earth. This crisis contributes to a greater issue in our identity which ultimately affects our pursuit of our purpose. When women leaders realize the power we have because we are in the kingdom of God, we will begin to walk out our purpose with more clarity and boldness than ever before.

TAKE ACTION

Be a god in the earth with a God identity.

Be a creator (create, develop, produce unique things in the earth).

Rule over God's creation in the earth.

Have dominion in the earth in your designated sphere of influence.

AFFIRMATION

I am made in God's image and I have authority in the earth. I will use my authority to dominate in my purpose.

THOUGHTS FOR YOUR JOURNAL

What is God's greater purpose for mankind?
What did He create us to do?

DAY 1 PRAYER POINTS

Father God, help me to be aware of your presence and our greater purpose. Forgive me for focusing on what I want and don't want. I know that I am here in this earth to glorify you. I will use my authority now to dominate and You will get the glory.

YOUR DAY 1 PRAYER POINTS

PRAYER STRATEGY

Which strategy did God give you in prayer?

OTHER REFERENCE: SCRIPTURES ABOUT GOD'S GREATER PURPOSE FOR MANKIND:

UNLEASHED TO LEAD (LEADERSHIP APPLICATION)

How will today's challenge impact you in your specific leadership role (i.e, business, career, politics, mother, wife, etc.)?

IMPACT

How does today impact your peace?

_____
_____
_____
_____
_____
_____
_____
_____
_____
_____
_____

QUOTE OF THE DAY

« If you believe you're supposed to follow all the time, then follow on; the world is full of people who will be more than happy to lead you. "

- Dr. Myles Munroe

SELF-CARE FOR PEACE TIP

Do not check any social media today. Take a break and focus on today's strategy.

Dr. Myles Munroe, Rediscovering the Kingdom: Ancient Hope for Our 21st Century World, (Destiny Images Publishers, Inc., 2010), 59.

Describe yourself as a leader.
Objectively evaluate yourself as a leader.
Describe how you manage your emotions.
Describe how you align your behavior with your values (Do you act like what you say you believe?).
Describe your understanding of how others perceive you (self-awareness).

Day 2: KNOW THE RESOURCES YOU HAVE

Psalm 115:14-16 (KJV) "The Lord shall increase you more and more, you and your children. Ye are blessed of the Lord which made heaven and earth. The heaven, even the heavens, are the Lord's: but the earth hath he given to the children of men."

ABOUT DAY 2

We often struggle with the idea that God will increase us. We have no peace because many of us worry about money and resources. We have been held back in our purpose because of "lack." We've stayed in unhealthy relationships and toxic careers because we don't realize the resources we have because of the God we serve. We belong to Him and He will prosper us more and more.

TAKE ACTION

Identify opportunities for you to have access to more (increase).

Identify areas in which God can add to what you already have and cause you to flourish.

Describe how you can further your leadership, career, ministry, nonprofit, etc.

AFFIRMATION

I have access to the world's resources because I belong to God and He gives to me and prospers me more and more and more.

THOUGHTS FOR YOUR JOURNAL

What does your life look like when you flourish
or when you are increased?
Describe it.

_____
_____
_____
_____
_____
_____
_____
_____
_____
_____
_____
_____
_____
_____
_____
_____
_____
_____
_____
_____
_____
_____
_____
_____
_____

DAY 2 PRAYER POINTS

Father God, help me to know You better and realize that because I belong to a God who is rich that I have all the resources I will need. Help me to move forward in faith that you will prosper me and give me what I need and desire.

YOUR DAY 2 PRAYER POINTS

PRAYER STRATEGY

Which strategy did God give you in prayer?

OTHER REFERENCE SCRIPTURES ABOUT KNOW THE RESOURCES YOU HAVE:

_____

_____

_____

_____

_____

UNLEASHED TO LEAD (LEADERSHIP APPLICATION)

As a leader in your current role, how will you use the resources you now know that you have?

_____

_____

_____

_____

_____

_____

_____

_____

_____

_____

_____

_____

_____

_____

_____

_____

_____

_____

QUOTE OF THE DAY

" Money can't manifest in a condition of survival. "

- Dr. Venus Opal Reese

SELF-CARE FOR PEACE TIP

Take a 10-15 min walk during your break and focus your mind on today's strategy.

Identify Human Resources (Coaches, Mentors, Spiritual Parents) and how they support your leadership.	Identify Technology/ Software Resources and how you can use them to develop your leadership.	Identify Monetary Resources and how much you can allocate to developing your leadership.	Identify Community Resources that you can use to help expand your brand.

IMPACT

How does today impact your peace?

_____

_____

_____

_____

_____

_____

_____

Dr. Venus Opal Reese, The Black Woman Millionaire: A Revolutionary Act That Defies Impossible, (Dr. Venus Opal Reese, 2018), 8.

Day 3: SEEK THE KINGDOM, THEN YOUR PURPOSE

Matthew 6:31-34 (AMPC) "But if God so clothes the grass of the field, which today is alive and green and tomorrow is tossed into the furnace, will He not much more surely clothe you, O you of little faith? Therefore do not worry and be anxious, saying, What are we going to have to eat? or, What are we going to have to drink? or, What are we going to have to wear? For the Gentiles (heathen) wish for and crave and diligently seek all these things, and your heavenly Father knows well that you need them all. But seek aim at and strive after) first of all His kingdom and His righteousness His way of doing and being right), and then all these things taken together will be given you besides. So do not worry or be anxious about tomorrow, for tomorrow will have worries and anxieties of its own. Sufficient for each day is its own trouble."

ABOUT DAY 3

God must be our number one priority through Jesus Christ (Yeshua). But when we aim after Him first, we still must aim after our kingdom purpose. We shouldn't be held back by worrying and stressing about our basic needs. But day by day pursue God and our kingdom purpose. Kingdom wealth is yours.

TAKE ACTION

Act as an ambassador for the kingdom.

Manifest God's image: operate in the god-class, act like God, copy Him, copy His moral nature, do His will, be the salt and the light.

Seek Him for His purpose to be fulfilled in your life then plan your life accordingly.

Rely on God to give you everything you need.

AFFIRMATION

Affirmation: God is my first priority and my kingdom purpose on the earth is God's priority for me. I will pursue Him, my purpose, and my prosperity every day.

How will you seek the kingdom first and then seek your purpose and prosperity?

Create a self-portrait of your new future.

Write seven reasons you will pursue your purpose this year.

Who is your hero (a woman leader in your industry)? Which traits do you admire and want to emulate?

_____

_____

_____

_____

_____

_____

_____

_____

_____

_____

_____

_____

_____

_____

_____

_____

_____

_____

_____

_____

_____

_____

_____

_____

_____

_____

_____

DAY 3 PRAYER POINTS

Father God, help me to seek after You and Your righteousness and pursue my kingdom purpose. Teach me how to prioritize and make You number one in my life. Help me to stop chasing the things that already belong to me and realign my actions and refocus on You.

YOUR DAY 3 PRAYER POINTS

PRAYER STRATEGY

Which strategy did God give you in prayer?

_____
_____
_____
_____
_____
_____
_____
_____
_____
_____
_____
_____
_____
_____
_____
_____
_____
_____

OTHER REFERENCE SCRIPTURES ABOUT SEEK THE KINGDOM, THEN YOUR PURPOSE:

UNLEASHED TO LEAD (LEADERSHIP APPLICATION)

As a leader in your current role, make a list of the things that have to change in your daily schedule and in your mindset to make God a priority.

DEMONSTRATE

Make Changes to Align with the Kingdom	
Identify the changes you will make in your thinking	Identify the changes you will make in your relationships
Identify the changes you will make in your finances	Identify the changes you will make in your profession

Extending the Strategy: Integrity

God is calling women leaders to a higher standard of integrity. If we say we're going to do something we need to do it. Some of us don't have peace because we haven't been operating with integrity. Define integrity. Identify areas in which you may have lacked integrity. Repent and keep moving forward in peace.

QUOTE OF THE DAY

❝ You will always act like the person you think you are.❞

- Dr. Mike Murdock

SELF-CARE FOR PEACE TIP

Send yourself 5 messages today on your phone about how amazing you are.

IMPACT

How does today impact your peace?

_____
_____
_____
_____
_____
_____
_____
_____
_____
_____
_____
_____
_____
_____
_____
_____

Dr. Mike Murdock, 7 Laws You Must Honor to Have Uncommon Success, (Deborah Murdock Johnson, 2010), 20.

Day 4: DETERMINE GOD'S PURPOSE FOR YOU

Proverbs 19:21 (AMPC) "Many plans are in a man's mind, but it is the Lord's purpose for him that will stand."

ABOUT DAY 4

I really and truly believe that God will bless whatever we set our hands to do. But I also believe that when we meditate on the Word day and night and develop our relationship with God, we will know our purpose more clearly before we set our hands to do anything. Then when we make our plans, our plans will align with God's purpose. He reveals to us through our relationship with Him.

TAKE ACTION

Operate in your kingdom purpose.

Pay attention to the signs and the prophetic that God has already revealed about your purpose.

Stay in close relationship with God so you can hear His voice regarding your purpose now through prayer, fasting, and reading His Word.

AFFIRMATION

I will meditate on the Word, pray, fast, and listen to God as He reveals His purpose for me. I will align my plans with His purpose.

THOUGHTS FOR YOUR JOURNAL

What is God's specific purpose for you?
How will you begin to execute your plans now?

_____

_____

_____

_____

_____

_____

_____

_____

_____

_____

_____

_____

_____

_____

_____

_____

_____

_____

_____

_____

_____

_____

_____

_____

_____

_____

_____

_____

_____

DAY 4 PRAYER POINTS

Father God, help me to hear you clearly about the direction you will have me to go. I have so many amazing plans that I know you will prosper but I want the plans You have for me. I believe I've heard you in my prayer time and through prophecy but make your purpose clear to me in this season.

YOUR DAY 4 PRAYER POINTS

PRAYER STRATEGY

Which strategy did God give you in prayer?

_____
_____
_____
_____
_____

UNLEASHED TO LEAD (LEADERSHIP APPLICATION)

Listen intently today. Write down all you hear Holy Spirit saying today. But then, write down all the prophecies you hear and see from others today. What do people ask you to do? How will you use what you hear and see to improve your leadership?

_____
_____
_____
_____
_____
_____
_____
_____
_____
_____
_____
_____
_____
_____
_____
_____

GETTING THE PICTURE: TRACK YOUR PURPOSE

Create a timeline to cover the following age ranges: 0-5; 6-11; 12-15; 16-18; 19-24; 25-35; 35+. At each of these stages, how did God begin to reveal your purpose to you?

IMPACT

How does today impact your peace?

_____
_____
_____
_____
_____
_____
_____
_____
_____
_____
_____
_____
_____
_____
_____
_____
_____
_____
_____

QUOTE OF THE DAY

❝ People don't approach the creation of success as a must-have obligation, do-or-die mission, gotta-have-it, 'hungry-dog-on-the-back-of-a-meat-truck' mentality. Then they spend the rest of their lives making excuses for why they didn't get it. ❞

-Grant Cardone

SELF-CARE FOR PEACE TIP

Take a nice bubble bath and relax your mind.

Grant Cardone, The 10X Rule: The Only Difference Between Success and Failure, (John Wiley & Sons, Inc., 2011), 27.

Day 5: IDENTIFY THE GOOD WORKS GOD CREATED FOR YOU

Ephesians 2:10 (AMPC) "For we are God's [own] handiwork (His workmanship), recreated in Christ Jesus, [born anew] that we may do those good works which God predestined (planned beforehand) for us [taking paths which He prepared ahead of time], that we should walk in them [living the good life which He prearranged and made ready for us to live]."

ABOUT DAY 5

God took pride in creating you and He uniquely created you to do something specific in the earth right now. He literally prepared a path for you to take and prearranged things for you so you can live the good life. You can choose the path He prepared or take the easy way out. Your good works will lead you to the good life – if you let them.

TAKE ACTION

List the gifts, talents, and skills God gave you.

Pay attention to the works that come naturally and spiritually for you and the fruit you've produced as a result.

Pay attention to the works that you've been doing since you were younger.

Do the good works and expect to live the good life that God already prearranged for you to live.

AFFIRMATION

I believe that my good works God created me to do will lead me on the path to the good life God has for me. I'm living my life like it's golden.

THOUGHTS FOR YOUR JOURNAL

What are the specific works God created you
to do?
What are your strengths and weaknesses?
What are 3 ways you can level up your works?

DAY 5 PRAYER POINTS

Father God, help me get on the path that you already prearranged for me. But God, help me not to veer off the path in any other directions. Even when obstacles are on the path, your joy is my strength. Help me to do the kind of works that produce much "good" fruit. Prepare my mindset for the good life you have for me.

YOUR DAY 5 PRAYER POINTS

PRAYER STRATEGY

Which strategy did God give you in prayer?

OTHER REFERENCE SCRIPTURES ABOUT IDENTIFY THE GOOD WORKS GOD CREATED FOR YOU:

UNLEASHED TO LEAD (LEADERSHIP APPLICATION)

How will you know when you are producing good fruit in your purpose? Describe what good fruit is in your area of leadership.

GETTING THE PICTURE: CHECK YOUR CIRCLE.

Create two concentric circles. Describe who is in your inner and outer circle and what they bring to the relationship.

IMPACT

How does today impact your peace?

_____
_____
_____
_____
_____
_____
_____
_____
_____
_____
_____
_____
_____
_____
_____
_____
_____
_____
_____
_____

QUOTE OF THE DAY

" Even those who lead masses of people must have a small inner core of followers who receive special attention. A leader who keeps everyone at arm's length never accomplishes the maximum. "

-Bob Briner & Ray Pritcher

SELF-CARE FOR PEACE TIP

Light a candle in your favorite fragrance and listen to uplifting music.

Bob Briner and Ray Pritchard, The Leadership Lessons of Jesus: A Timeless Model for Today's Leaders, (B & H Publishing Group, 2008), 31.

Day 6: KNOW WHERE YOUR PEACE COMES FROM

John 14:27 (AMPC) "Peace I leave with you; My [own] peace I now give and bequeath to you. Not as the world gives do I give to you. Do not let your hearts be troubled, neither let them be afraid. [Stop allowing yourselves to be agitated and disturbed; and do not permit yourselves to be fearful and intimidated and cowardly and unsettled.]"

ABOUT DAY 6

One of the biggest fights of my life was for the peace that Yeshua already gave to me. I allowed the devil to lie to me because of a tragedy I experienced in my life. Yeshua doesn't give peace as the world gives it and takes it away. Our peace is constant even if the events in our lives are not. No matter what you experience in life or leadership, hold on to your peace.

TAKE ACTION

Receive the gift of peace directly from Yeshua (Jesus Christ).

Keep your peace because it is your birthright, your inheritance.

Maintain your peace, love, power, and a sound mind because they belong to you - fear is a spirit that comes from the devil.

Keep your peace because peace makes purpose possible.

Don't be anxious, worried, agitated, disturbed, cowardly, intimidated or unsettled because you have peace.

AFFIRMATION

I will not allow even the most tragic events in my life to rob me of my peace. I will tell God what I want and need and maintain my peace that He will do it.

THOUGHTS FOR YOUR JOURNAL

Where does your peace come from?
According to the John 14:27, whose peace did you receive?
Why should you always have peace?
What are 3 major moves you can make to mainain your peace and keep moving forward in your purpose?

_____

_____

_____

_____

_____

_____

_____

_____

_____

_____

_____

_____

_____

_____

_____

_____

_____

_____

_____

_____

_____

_____

_____

_____

DAY 6 PRAYER POINTS

Father God, help me to hold on to my peace. The attacks have been frequent and strategic but I have power on the inside of me. I know where my peace comes from. I know I have power over all the power of the enemy but sometimes I get weak. I thank You for Your strength and the gift of peace.

YOUR DAY 6 PRAYER POINTS

PRAYER STRATEGY

Which strategy did God give you in prayer?

OTHER REFERENCE SCRIPTURES ABOUT KNOW WHERE YOUR PEACE COMES FROM:

_____
_____
_____
_____
_____

UNLEASHED TO LEAD (LEADERSHIP APPLICATION)

What are you allowing to threaten your peace?
How will you change this?

_____
_____
_____
_____
_____
_____
_____
_____
_____
_____
_____
_____
_____
_____
_____
_____
_____
_____
_____

EXTENDING THE STRATEGY: VISION

Write a vision statement for you and your leadership. Create a visual image (graph, map, chart, picture) that depicts your vision.

IMPACT

How does today impact your peace?

_____
_____
_____
_____
_____
_____
_____
_____
_____
_____
_____
_____
_____
_____
_____
_____
_____
_____
_____
_____
_____
_____

QUOTE OF THE DAY

" The enemy has launched major assignments against women to shut down the call of God on their lives."

-Kimberly Daniels

SELF-CARE FOR PEACE TIP

Get a massage, manicure and/or pedicure today.

Bob Briner and Ray Pritchard, The Leadership Lessons of Jesus: A Timeless Model for Today's Leaders, (B & H Publishing Group, 2008), 31.

Day 7: PRAY AND SEEK GOD FOR CLARITY

Colossians 1:15-16 (MSG) "We look at this Son and see the God who cannot be seen. We look at this Son and see God's original purpose in everything created. For everything, absolutely everything, above and below, visible and invisible, rank after rank after rank of angels— everything got started in him and finds its purpose in him. He was there before any of it came into existence and holds it all together right up to this moment. And when it comes to the church, he organizes and holds it together, like a head does a body."

ABOUT DAY 7

The revelation in this scripture amazes me. But the part that really stretched me is "everything got started and finds its purpose in Him." We have been getting it wrong for so long. If the way we find our purpose is in Jesus and we don't have a relationship with Jesus, no wonder we haven't had peace about our purpose. Now is our opportunity to get closer to Jesus and ask Him if we're anywhere close to finding our purpose in Him.

TAKE ACTION

Jesus to determine the purpose for which mankind was created.

Find your purpose in your relationship with Jesus.

Determine how you will make Jesus the head of your life.

Explore how everything in the earth was created for Jesus.

Ask yourself questions daily about alignment: Are my actions/decisions aligned with God's purpose? Is my thinking/mindset conductive for legendary leadership? Does my effort match my mission?

AFFIRMATION

I will not allow myself to get caught up in me. I will seek Jesus for His purpose for me and I will be faithful in fulfilling it.

36

THOUGHTS FOR YOUR JOURNAL

When you look at Jesus, describe how you see Jesus both as
the Son of Man and as God?
What is your God-given purpose?
How do you know this is your God-given purpose?

DAY 7 PRAYER POINTS

Father God, I want to be able to see Jesus more clearly as God. My purpose can only be found in Jesus so help me find Him so I can have clarity about my purpose. I'm tired of dead ends. I'm tired of struggling financially. I'm tired of starting and stopping. Teach me how to understand Your kingdom and your kingdom purpose for me.

YOUR DAY 7 PRAYER POINTS

PRAYER STRATEGY

Which strategy did God give you in prayer?

OTHER REFERENCE SCRIPTURES ABOUT PRAY AND SEEK GOD FOR CLARITY:

_____

_____

_____

_____

_____

QUOTE

" I have peace in knowing that God has a greater purpose for mankind and I fit perfectly in His kingdom plan. "

UNLEASHED TO LEAD (LEADERSHIP APPLICATION)

As a leader, you must make sure that you're leading according to your purpose. Is your leadership representative of the kingdom? How are you teaching your followers to understand their purpose?

_____

_____

_____

_____

_____

_____

_____

_____

_____

_____

_____

_____

GETTING THE PICTURE: MANIFESTING YOUR PEACE

MANIFESTING MY PEACE IN MY PURPOSE

What does it look like when I have peace in my purpose?

1	2	3	4	5
No People Bondage	No fears or anxieties	No stagnancy	Violent Pursuit	Definiteness of Purpose
No one has to agree with you or confirm you. You won't stop no matter what they say.	You use the Word of God to destroy spirits of fear and anxiety and strongholds.	You no longer get stuck and stay stuck. You seek a coach, mentor, and accountability partner.	In the same way that you seek God - early in the morning, continuously, you seek your purpose like your life depends on it.	You know who you are and what you were created to do and you won't ever quit. You speak your purpose with conviction.

NO PEOPLE BONDAGE	No one has to agree with you or confirm you. You won't stop no matter what they say.
NO FEARS OR ANXIETIES	You use the Word of God to destroy spirits of fear and anxiety and strongholds.
NO STAGNANCY	You no longer get stuck and stay stuck. You seek a coach, mentor, and accountability partner.
VIOLENT PURSUIT	In the same way that you seek God - early in the morning, continuously, you seek your purpose like your life depends on it.
DEFINITENESS OF PURPOSE	You know who you are and what you were created to do and you won't ever quit. You speak your purpose with conviction.

IMPACT

How does today impact your peace?

_____

_____

_____

_____

_____

_____

_____

_____

_____

_____

_____

_____

_____

_____

_____

_____

_____

_____

_____

QUOTE OF THE DAY

« Seek clarity on who you want to be, how you
want to interact with others, what you
want, and what will bring you the greatest meaning." »

-Brendon Burchard

SELF-CARE FOR PEACE TIP

**Write yourself a "celebrate me" list at the end of today to celebrate
yourself and your accomplishments.**

WEEK ONE REVIEW

Today, pray and seek God for clarity about His purpose and your plans. You were created for His glory. Does He get glory from your leadership? Write what God gives you. Make sure you are in alignment with His purpose for you. How has week one impacted your peace. Receive His peace as you fulfill your purpose.

LEADERSHIP PROFILE:

What changes have you seen in yourself?	What mindset changes have you seen?	How do you react differently to different situations?

*Brendon Burchard, High Performance Habits: How Extraordinary People Become That Way
(Hay House, Inc., 2017), 37.*

WEEK2

MAKING
Progress
IN YOUR
Purpose

Day 8: BE PRODUCTIVE, INCREASE, AND BECOME GREATER

Genesis 1:27-28 (AMPC) "So God created man in His own image, in the image and likeness of God He created him; male and female He created them. And God blessed them and said to them, Be fruitful, multiply, and fill the earth, and subdue it [using all its vast resources in the service of God and man]; and have dominion over the fish of the sea, the birds of the air, and over every living creature that moves upon the earth."

ABOUT DAY 8

If I knew at age 14 what I know now, oh my life and my son's life would have been different. From the beginning, we were "blessed" and instructed to 1) be fruitful, 2) multiply, 3) fill the earth, 4) subdue the earth, and 5) have dominion over it. Now that we know that God "blessed" us to fulfill our purpose, nothing should be able to stop our progress. God gave us the command "be." So, leader I want to challenge you to always "be" in a state of productivity. I challenge you to develop your capacity to create products and services that yield kingdom results.

TAKE ACTION

Define what fruitfulness looks like in your area of leadership.

Create a formula for multiplication in your finances and leadership: increase the number of followers, number of leaders you develop, products and services, franchises, and souls for Jesus.

Determine how you will fill the earth with kingdom leadership (i.e., city, state, region, nation, internationally).

Create a plan to dominate in your sphere of influence.

AFFIRMATION

I will continuously create products, services, and programs for my followers that yield kingdom results.

How fruitful is your leadership?
Are people being set free? Are the oppressed being delivered? Explain.
Is what you're developing in other leaders being duplicated? Explain.
Are you using all the resources God has available to you? Explain.
Are you taking back everything you lost? Explain.
Are you ruling and dominating in your sphere of leadership? Explain

_____

_____

_____

_____

_____

_____

_____

_____

_____

_____

_____

_____

_____

_____

_____

_____

_____

_____

_____

_____

_____

_____

_____

DAY 8 PRAYER POINTS

Father God, I want to make continual progress in my kingdom purpose. I want momentum in my career, finances, and spiritual life. I want the work I do with my hands to be productive. I want my leadership to yield abundance in my life and in the kingdom.

YOUR DAY 8 PRAYER POINTS

PRAYER STRATEGY

Which strategy did God give you in prayer?

OTHER REFERENCES SCRIPTURES ABOUT BE PRODUCTIVE, INCREASE, AND BECOME GREATER:

IMPACT

How does today impact your progress?

UNLEASHED TO LEAD (LEADERSHIP APPLICATION)

As a leader, you must make sure that you're fruitful. Think of all the things that have hindered you from being fruitful up to this point. Make a list of all the obstacles. Make a plan for how you will combat any obstacle that tries to block you from moving forward.

DEMONSTRATE

Action Plan Template: Create 10-year goals for the work of your hands.			
Goal	Timeline	Status	Resources Needed

QUOTE OF THE DAY

66 If I asked you about your current financial status, could you, right now, list on a blank piece of paper all your assets and liabilities, including your investments, bank accounts, mortgages, and credit card debts? **99**

- David Bach

David Bach, Smart Women Finish Rich: 9 Steps to Achieving Financial Security and Funding Your Dreams (Broadway Books, 1999), 57.

Day 9: STRONG AND BOLD IN PURSUIT OF YOUR PURPOSE

Joshua 1:7-9 (AMPC) "Only you be strong and very courageous, that you may do according to all the law which Moses My servant commanded you. Turn not from it to the right hand or to the left, that you may prosper wherever you go. This Book of the Law shall not depart out of your mouth, but you shall meditate on it day and night, that you may observe and do according to all that is written in it. For then you shall make your way prosperous, and then you shall deal wisely and have good success. Have not I commanded you? Be strong, vigorous, and very courageous. Be not afraid, neither be dismayed, for the Lord your God is with you wherever you go."

ABOUT DAY 9

Don't play with it any more. God is calling us out of timidity, shyness, insecurity, inconsistency, and inadequacy. God is calling us – no He is commanding us to be strong and bold in pursuit of the purpose He prearranged for us. His Word is the guide we need to boldly pursue our destiny. But you must read His Word, focus on it, meditate, on it day and night, and speak it over your own life. This is the way to prosper yourself. You don't need any more confirmation. Boldly. Pursue. Your. Destiny.

TAKE ACTION

Establish a study schedule and meditate on His Word both day and night.

Identify everything that has caused you to be afraid and/or intimidated in the past.

Describe how your purpose will prosper you.

Identify areas in which you need to obey God's Word.

Describe what "good success" is in your area of leadership.

AFFIRMATION

I will be strong and boldly pursue my purpose. I will meditate on the Word day and night. I will make my own way prosperous, have wisdom and have good success.

THOUGHTS FOR YOUR JOURNAL

How can you improve your physical health to be stronger physically?
How can you improve your mindset to be stronger mentally?
How can you become more courageous in the pursuit of your purpose?
Are you using all the resources God has available to you? Explain.

DAY 9 PRAYER POINTS

Father God, help me keep my consistency in reading your Word and meditating on it day and night. Increase my desire to know You more. Increase my capacity to read and speak Your Word over my life and my leadership for You. Help me to balance my reliance on You and my responsibility for making my own way prosperous.

YOUR DAY 9 PRAYER POINTS

PRAYER STRATEGY

Which strategy did God give you in prayer?

OTHER REFERENCE SCRIPTURES ABOUT BE STRONG AND BOLD IN PURSUIT:

_____

UNLEASHED TO LEAD (LEADERSHIP APPLICATION)

As a leader, be bolder in your prayers. In which areas do you need to be stronger and bolder? What has caused you to stop pursuing or be stagnant in pursuing your purpose?
Make a list of all the things you need to have good success in leadership. Utilize your angels, ministering spirits to go get what you need to be successful in leadership.

_____

DEMONSTRATE

Action Plan Template: Create five-year courageous and bold goals			
Goal	Timeline	Status	Resources Needed

IMPACT

How does today impact your progress?

_____

_____

_____

_____

_____

_____

_____

QUOTE OF THE DAY

❝ The enemy will always seek to hinder you in areas where you are keeping his goals from being accomplished…Satan will predictably want to cripple you in the area of your life where doing so will most directly defame God and hinder his church. ❞

- Priscilla Shirer

Priscilla Shirer, The Armor of God, (Lifeway Press, 2015), 30.

Day 10: BE HAPPY AND BLESSED IN YOUR PURSUIT

Psalm 1:1-3 (AMPC) "Blessed (happy, fortunate, prosperous, and enviable) is the man who walks and lives not in the counsel of the ungodly [following their advice, their plans and purposes], nor stands [submissive and inactive] in the path where sinners walk, nor sits down [to relax and rest where the scornful [and the mockers] gather. But his delight and desire are in the law of the Lord, and on His law (the precepts, the instructions, the teachings of God) he habitually meditates (ponders and studies) by day and by night. And he shall be like a tree firmly planted [and tended] by the streams of water, ready to bring forth its fruit in its season; its leaf also shall not fade or wither; and everything he does shall prosper [and come to maturity]."

ABOUT DAY 10

This scripture screams two main points for how we can be blessed (happy, fortunate, prosperous, and enviable): 1) check your circle and 2) meditate on and delight in the Word day and night. What happens leaders when we follow these two steps? Our leadership assignments are secured. But not only that, our leadership will produce the kind of fruit that causes us to prosper. Everything you do will prosper. That's huge! How many of you have evaluated your circle lately? Are you taking counsel from ungodly, carnal, or worldly people? Also, I have so many women leaders who have invested in coaching and courses with me and it is difficult for some of them to stay consistent enough to make progress. Are you really ready to be happy and blessed in your pursuit of your purpose?

TAKE ACTION

Rearrange your daily schedule to maximize your time.

Analyze your current personal circle, professional circle, religious circle, and/or social circle.

Describe how you are motivated to make progress.

Describe how your life and leadership will look in 10 years because of the changes you make today.

AFFIRMATION

I will be strategic in whom I allow to speak into me. I will make it my duty to meditate on the Word of God day and night. Everything I do shall prosper.

Are people (ungodly, scornful, sinners) holding you back from your happiness and your progress?
How will you evaluate your associations?

DAY 10 PRAYER POINTS

Father God, help me to walk and live in my purpose. Help me to take a stand for what is right. Help me to understand my position, seated in heavenly places in Christ Jesus. Help me to take delight in studying Your Word so I can make progress in my purpose.

YOUR DAY 10 PRAYER POINTS

PRAYER STRATEGY

Which strategy did God give you in prayer?

UNLEASHED TO LEAD (LEADERSHIP APPLICATION)

As a leader, people follow your steps. It is important to have your priorities in order. Complete a schedule for your day to help you to be more structured in meditating on the Word.

DEMONSTRATE

Action Plan Template: Create your three-year goals.			
Goal	Timeline	Status	Resources Needed

GETTING THE PICTURE: PRIORITIZING

FIT EVERYTHING ELSE IN YOUR SCHEDULE					
TIME	MON	TUES	WED	THURS	FRI
6:30AM	Study passage & pray	Study passage & pray	Study passage & pray	Study passage & pray	Study passage & pray
7:00AM					
7:30AM					
8:00AM					
8:30AM					
9:00AM					
9:30AM					

10:00AM					
10:30AM					
11:00AM					
11:30AM					
12:00PM	Meditate on the passage & listen to God	Meditate on the passage & listen to God	Meditate on the passage & listen to God	Meditate on the passage & listen to God	Meditate on the passage & listen to God
12:30PM	Journal	Journal	Journal	Journal	Journal
1:00PM					
1:30PM					
2:00PM					
2:30PM					
3:00PM					
3:30PM					
3:30PM					

4:00PM					
4:30PM					

IMPACT

How does today impact your progress?

_____
_____
_____
_____
_____
_____
_____
_____
_____
_____
_____
_____
_____
_____
_____
_____
_____
_____

QUOTE OF THE DAY

❝ You will always feel out of balance if you're doing work that you don't find engaging and meaningful... **❞**

-Brendon Burchard

Brendon Burchard, High Performance Habits: How Extraordinary People Become That Way (Hay House, Inc., 2017), 37.

Day 11: OBEY AND MOVE FORWARD

Deuteronomy 28:1-2 (AMPC) "If you will listen diligently to the voice of the Lord your God, being watchful to do all His commandments which I command you this day, the Lord your God will set you high above all the nations of the earth. And all these blessings shall come upon you and overtake you if you heed the voice of the Lord your God."

ABOUT DAY 11

No matter how we look at the Word, how we try to analyze it or how much we ignore it, we won't be able to avoid being obedient to God's Word. We can't run from His continual compelling us to read it and obey it. We often want the blessings without the obedience and we want the rewards without the relationship. We want to be set high – the promotion but in order to make continual progress, and for the blessings to overtake us, we must read His Word and obey it.

TAKE ACTION

Establish a study schedule and meditate on His Word both day and night.

Identify the strongholds in your mind that have caused you to miss God and your blessings.

Describe where you're going so you can make progress toward that place.

Describe what your promotion looks like in this season; the next five years; and the next ten years.

AFFIRMATION

All the blessings will overtake me and God will promote me because I listen diligently to His voice and I read and obey His Word.

THOUGHTS FOR YOUR JOURNAL

Where is your destiny (purpose, calling, position, assignment in life) destination?
Where will your purpose land you specifically?
How will you know when you've arrived?

_____

_____

_____

_____

_____

_____

_____

_____

_____

_____

_____

_____

_____

_____

_____

_____

_____

_____

_____

_____

_____

_____

_____

_____

_____

DAY 11 PRAYER POINTS

Father God, help me see the map you've created for my life. Help me know the destination for my destiny. When my way seems dark and my leadership is obscure, help me stay in the Word so my mind can be renewed and I will know your acceptable will for my life.

YOUR DAY 11 PRAYER POINTS

PRAYER STRATEGY

Which strategy did God give you in prayer?

OTHER REFERENCE SCRIPTURES ABOUT OBEY AND MOVE FORWARD:

UNLEASHED TO LEAD (LEADERSHIP APPLICATION)

As a leader, reflecting on from where you came can help ensure that you do or don't repeat some of the same actions. Make a list of how you've been able to maintain continual movement in your leadership (career). Are there childhood or generational habits that have held you back? What are they? Are there powerful habits that have kept you moving forward?

DEMONSTRATE

Action Plan Template: Create quarterly goals that will help you reach your annual goals.				
Goal	Motivation	Timeline	Status	Resources Needed
Quarter 1:				
Quarter 2:				
Quarter 3				
Quarter 4:				

PICTURE THIS: MAP IT OUT
Create a map that depicts where you're going in your purpose.

IMPACT

How does today impact your progress?

_____
_____
_____
_____
_____
_____
_____
_____
_____
_____
_____
_____
_____
_____
_____

QUOTE OF THE DAY

"We won't see maximum results of intensity in prayer until we become more effective in the way we pray. And we won't be as effective in prayer until we add intensity in the way we pray."

-Apostle Jonathan Ferguson

Apostle Jonathan Ferguson, Bootcamp Prayer Revised, (Ferguson Global, 2015), 11-12.

Day 12: GO AND GOD WILL BLESS YOU

Genesis 12:1-3 (AMPC) "Now [in Haran] the Lord said to Abram, Go for yourself [for your own advantage] away from your country, from your relatives and your father's house, to the land that I will show you. And I will make of you a great nation, and I will bless you [with abundant increase of favors] and make your name famous and distinguished, and you will be a blessing [dispensing good to others]. And I will bless those who bless you [who confer prosperity or happiness upon you] and curse him who curses or uses insolent language toward you; in you will all the families and kindred of the earth be blessed [and by you they will bless themselves]."

ABOUT DAY 12

There are blessings tied to Abram's obedience and to his movement. God is either telling you to go or to stay but in this season, you have to do something. God will show you the destination. But sometimes He just wants you to get packed up. Your packing is your preparing for the destination. Stop waiting on something to happen and go ahead and start packing. Make preparations for the blessings. God is about to make your name famous and distinguish you and you will be even more of a blessing to those you lead. Your family and other families will be impacted when you obey and move.

TAKE ACTION

Write down where you hear God telling you to go.

You belong somewhere, not everywhere. Describe places you've felt you do not belong.

Describe the place that will nurture your growth and your progress.

Describe the place in which people will celebrate you and not tolerate you.

AFFIRMATION

I am willing to go or be still at God's command. God has land, territory, and real estate for me. God will make my name famous and distinguish me among leaders. If anyone comes against me, God will handle them for me.

THOUGHTS FOR YOUR JOURNAL

Your progress depends on whether or not you "go?"
Which steps will you take immediately so you can "go" and then be blessed?

_____

_____

_____

_____

_____

_____

_____

_____

_____

_____

_____

_____

_____

_____

_____

_____

_____

_____

_____

_____

_____

_____

_____

_____

_____

_____

_____

_____

DAY 12 PRAYER POINTS

Father God, help me to discern where I belong. Help me not to give up and leave a place I was created to possess. Prepare my heart and mind now to be able to handle the fame attached to my leadership assignment. My desire is to represent You and Your kingdom in excellence.

YOUR DAY 12 PRAYER POINTS

PRAYER STRATEGY

Which strategy did God give you in prayer?

OTHER REFERENCE SCRIPTURES ABOUT GO AND GOD WILL BLESS YOU:

_____

UNLEASHED TO LEAD (LEADERSHIP APPLICATION)

As a leader, your weakness will flourish and your strength will die if you stay when God has said to go. Describe how you are flourishing where you are in your leadership now.

_____

DEMONSTRATE

Action Plan Template: Create monthly goals with weekly milestones that will help you reach your quarterly goals.

Monthly Goal	Milestones	Obstacles That May Arise	Timeline	Resources Needed
Month 1	Week 1: Week 2: Week 3: Week 4:			
Month 2	Week 1: Week 2: Week 3: Week 4:			
Month 3	Week 1: Week 2: Week 3: Week 4:			

IMPACT

How does today impact your progress?

_____
_____
_____
_____
_____
_____
_____

QUOTE OF THE DAY

" Your assignment is always the problem God has assigned you to solve for others. "

-Dr. Mike Murdock

Dr. Mike Murdock, 7 Laws You Must Honor to Have Uncommon Success, (Deborah Murdock Johnson, 2010), 31.

Day 13: PRESS TOWARD YOUR MARK AND THE MARK

Philippians 3:13-15 (AMPC) "I do not consider, brethren, that I have captured and made it my own [yet]; but one thing I do [it is my one aspiration]: forgetting what lies behind and straining forward to what lies ahead, I press on toward the goal to win the [supreme and heavenly] prize to which God in Christ Jesus is calling us upward. So let those [of us] who are spiritually mature and full-grown have this mind and hold these convictions; and if in any respect you have a different attitude of mind, God will make that clear to you also."

ABOUT DAY 13

What if your past includes the death of your child? Job loss? Public humiliation? Do you still forget the things that are behind you? Your progress will forever be paralyzed if you don't decide right now to forget the things behind you and strain forward to what lies ahead. God has a plan for you and not just the heavenly one, the ultimate prize of your salvation. God also has a future plan to prosper you right here on earth but you must press forward. It's a mindset though. Some women leaders aren't spiritually mature enough to hold this conviction. They fall off and come back. They start and stop. They allow the past and even the present to paralyze them. Which woman leader are you?

TAKE ACTION

Explain the things that you haven't moved past yet.

Describe the earthly prize God has for you.

Make a plan for how you will move forward and make progress.

AFFIRMATION

I am the type of woman who will move forward beyond the grief and hurt and press toward the blessings God has for me.

THOUGHTS FOR YOUR JOURNAL

What are some of the obstacles that are pressing against your progress?
Describe how you will "press" toward your purpose and God's purpose.

_____

_____

_____

_____

_____

_____

_____

_____

_____

_____

_____

_____

_____

_____

_____

_____

_____

_____

_____

_____

_____

_____

_____

_____

_____

DAY 13 PRAYER POINTS

Father God, I know I'm an overcomer but I need some supernatural support to help me overcome. I need help renewing my mind so that I don't keep rehearsing the things that are behind me. Those things hurt me; shook me to my core. But I'm ready to press now. I'm ready for what lies ahead.

YOUR DAY 13 PRAYER POINTS

PRAYER STRATEGY

Which strategy did God give you in prayer?

_____
_____
_____
_____
_____
_____
_____
_____
_____
_____
_____
_____
_____
_____
_____

OTHER REFERENCE SCRIPTURES ABOUT PRESS TOWARD YOUR MARK AND THE MARK:

_____
_____
_____
_____
_____

UNLEASHED TO LEAD (LEADERSHIP APPLICATION)

As a leader, your people need you to press. Describe how your assignment helps other people who are in need of what you have.

_____
_____
_____
_____
_____
_____
_____
_____
_____
_____
_____
_____
_____
_____
_____
_____
_____

DEMONSTRATE

Describe your goal (mark)! How will you press toward it in spite of the obstacles?

Obstacle – Money >>>> Your Mark _____

Obstacle – Fear >>>>Your Mark _____

Obstacle – Lack of Support>>>> Your Mark _____

_____

_____

_____

_____

_____

_____

_____

_____

_____

IMPACT

How does today impact your progress?

_____

_____

_____

_____

_____

_____

_____

QUOTE OF THE DAY

" Faith in God and His Word that is acted upon will bring results every time."

- Kenneth Hagin

Kenneth Hagin, The Midas: A Balanced Approach to Biblical Prosperity,(Faith Library Publications, 2011), 31.

Day 14: GO AND FULFILL YOUR PURPOSE

Matthew 28:19-20 (AMPC) "Go then and make disciples of all the nations, baptizing them into the name of the Father and of the Son and of the Holy Spirit, Teaching them to observe everything that I have commanded you, and behold, I am with you all the days (perpetually, uniformly, and on every occasion), to the [very] close and consummation of the age. Amen (so let it be)."

ABOUT DAY 14

There is no progress without action. Yeshua (Jesus) gave us a mission that requires present action. You should always be in "go" mode. Yes, enter into His rest but don't rest too long. Go. Make. Baptize. Teach. This mission is universal for all kingdom leaders. In everything we do, we go, make, baptize, and teach. Our message whether explicit or implicit is "the kingdom of heaven is at hand." Jesus is with us in everything we do. We, however must allow Him and His Spirit to energize us to go. Start today.

TAKE ACTION

Use your marriage to fuel you to go as "married people have more energy than their never married counterparts."

Map out where you will go in this season and how you will expand the kingdom when you go.

Explain your individual mission and how it aligns with the mission of mankind.

AFFIRMATION

I will make sure I keep my energy levels high and not allow life's circumstances to zap me of my energy. Each and every day I will go.

Brendon Burchard, *High Performance Habits: How Extraordinary People Become That Way* (Hay House, Inc., 2017), 37.

THOUGHTS FOR YOUR JOURNAL

What has God given you to equip you when you go (concrete)?
What emotions and spirits have haunted you to prevent you from going?
How will you now move forward knowing Jesus said He is with you?

_____

_____

_____

_____

_____

_____

_____

_____

_____

_____

_____

_____

_____

_____

_____

_____

_____

_____

_____

_____

_____

_____

_____

_____

_____

DAY 14 PRAYER POINTS

Father God, I'm ready to go. Set me up now. Set me up mentally and help me develop a "Yes I Can" and "Nothing Can Stop Me" mindset. Set me up spiritually so I can be equipped to respond in life and leadership according to Your Spirit. Set me up physically. I want to prosper in health as my soul prospers so I can have the energy and physical stamina to go. Set me up financially so I can have all the resources and money I need to advance your kingdom and care for my family and friends. Thank You Jesus for going with me and leading me at the same time.

YOUR DAY 14 PRAYER POINTS

PRAYER STRATEGY

Which strategy did God give you in prayer?

OTHER REFERENCE SCRIPTURES ABOUT GO AND FULFILL YOUR PURPOSE:

_____
_____
_____
_____
_____

UNLEASHED TO LEAD (LEADERSHIP APPLICATION)

As a leader, you have to have the energy to "go." If our life circumstances aren't optimal, we often allow life to zap our energy. You must have an internal or intrinsic desire to go. Describe your level of physical energy and what you will do to improve it. Describe your level of spiritual energy (how you allow Holy Spirit to energize you, build you up, pull you off the bed of affliction). Describe your leadership energy level. Do you show up consistently?

_____
_____
_____
_____
_____
_____
_____
_____
_____
_____
_____
_____
_____
_____

IMPACT

How does today impact your progress?

_____
_____
_____
_____
_____
_____
_____
_____
_____
_____

QUOTE OF THE DAY

" The fundamentals of becoming more productive are setting goals and maintaining energy and focus. No goals, no focus, no energy – and you're dead in the water. Productivity starts with goals. When you have clear and challenging goals, you tend to be more focused and engaged… "

-Brendon Burchard

WEEK TWO REVIEW:

Today, pray and seek God for how to make daily continual progress in your purpose. Write the steps God gives you. Make sure you are in alignment with His purpose for you. Receive His peace.

LEADERSHIP PROFILE:

What changes have you seen in yourself?	What mindset changes have you seen?	How do you react differently to different situations?

MANIFESTATION

What has manifested in your life in the area of peace in your purpose?	What has manifested in your life in the area of progress in your purpose?

Brendon Burchard, High Performance Habits: How Extraordinary People Become That Way (Hay House, Inc., 2017), 177.

WEEK 3

ACHIEVING
Prosperity
IN YOUR
Purpose

Day 15: BE WILLING AND OBEDIENT

Isaiah 1:19 (AMPC) "If you are willing and obedient, you shall eat the good of the land."

ABOUT DAY 15

Wow! This scripture always blesses me and keeps me in check. Am I both willing and obedient? Are you? Sometimes we will do what God has called us to do but we have an attitude about it. We obey but really down inside we're mad or resentful. We will resign, relocate, leave him or take the demotion but we're bitter about having to do it. God wants you at a place of sweet surrender – a place at which you totally trust Him with your whole life. When we reach this place, we will be willing and obedient. Don't you want to eat the fruit of the land?

TAKE ACTION

Identify areas in which you've been unwilling.

Describe how you will rectify these areas.

Describe the good of the land for you and your leadership.

AFFIRMATION

I am willing to follow Jesus and His plan for my life. As He reveals my steps daily, I will obey. I will eat the fruit of the land.

THOUGHTS FOR YOUR JOURNAL

What is the source of your unwillingness and disobedience?
How does unwillingness and disobedience hinder your progress?
How are others impacted by your unwillingness and disobedience?

_____

_____

_____

_____

_____

_____

_____

_____

_____

_____

_____

_____

_____

_____

_____

_____

_____

_____

_____

_____

_____

_____

_____

_____

_____

_____

DAY 15 PRAYER POINTS

Father God, I admit that I've been disobedient or unwilling in some areas of my life. But I'm ready to get to that sweet place of surrender now. I'm ready to surrender my will, my way, my thoughts and align them with yours. I'm ready to eat the fruit of the land.

YOUR DAY 15 PRAYER POINTS

PRAYER STRATEGY

Which strategy did God give you in prayer?

OTHER REFERENCE SCRIPTURES ABOUT BE WILLING AND OBEDIENT:

_____
_____
_____
_____
_____

UNLEASHED TO LEAD (LEADERSHIP APPLICATION)

Most duplicity with money starts because of a lack of money or a love of money. Both are ungodly. As a leader, you need the cures for a lack of money so you can manage money better. Are you willing to make changes?

_____
_____
_____
_____
_____
_____
_____
_____
_____
_____
_____
_____
_____
_____
_____
_____

MANAGE WHAT YOU HAVE:

Seven Cures for a Lean Purse	Explanation	Action
1. Start thy purse to fattening.	Save a certain amount each day and 10% of your earnings.	
2. Control thy expenditures.	Budget your money and spend less than what you earn.	
3. Make thy gold multiply.	Save with interest; invest in real estate or other stocks.	
4. Guard thy treasures from loss	Research before investing; make sure it is a good investment.	
5. Make of thy dwelling a profitable investment.	Stop throwing money away on renting and make a plan to buy your own home.	
6. Insure a future income.	Make a retirement plan for when you stop working.	
7. Increase thy ability to earn.	Have multiple streams of income.	
Seven Cures for a Lean Purse from The Richest Man in Babylon (Clason, 1926)		

IMPACT

How does today impact your prosperity?

_____
_____
_____
_____
_____
_____
_____
_____
_____
_____
_____

QUOTE OF THE DAY

" "…God's Word is true… and if you're not eating the good of the land, it may be because you don't qualify. **"**

- Kenneth Hagin

Kenneth Hagin, The Midas Touch: A Balanced Approach to Biblical Prosperity,
(Faith Library Publications, 2011), 11

Day 16: MANAGE WHAT YOU HAVE

Luke 16:10 (AMPC) "He who is faithful in a very little [thing] is faithful also in much, and he who is dishonest and unjust in a very little [thing] is dishonest and unjust also in much. Therefore if you have not been faithful in the [case of] unrighteous mammon (deceitful riches, money, possessions), who will entrust to you the true riches? And if you have not proved faithful in that which belongs to another [whether God or man], who will give you that which is your own [that is, the true riches]?

ABOUT DAY 16

I repent! How many of us ask for more and more and more but we haven't been faithful in our stewardship over what we have. How many of us have had some shady dealings with the little we have? Income tax fraud (allowing someone to claim our child or claiming theirs)? Welfare fraud (buying or selling food stamps)? Fudging receipts? Mismanaging something that belongs to someone else? Any other shady dealings with money? This is our opportunity to repent because our money may have been cursed because of our duplicity. Management includes being a good steward – honest, upright, and just in our dealings with money. Manage what you have.

TAKE ACTION

Identify areas in which you've been faithful and unfaithful.

Describe your characteristics that qualify you for true riches.

Describe the things other people have entrusted to you and how you've been a good steward (or not) over those things.

AFFIRMATION

I will be honest, upright, and just in my dealings with money – mine and others' I am a good manager of what I have. I can save, sow, tithe, give, increase, and multiply the money God gives me.

THOUGHTS FOR YOUR JOURNAL

Do you have a budget?
How do you manage your money now?
How much debt do you have?
How do you need to manage your money, your business's money,
the organization's money better?
What steps will you take to manage money better?

DAY 16 PRAYER POINTS

Father God, I repent for not being faithful over that which you've given me. I'm ready now Lord. I want to be honest, upright, and just in my dealings with money. I break every financial curse in Jesus's name – even those I brought upon myself.

YOUR DAY 16 PRAYER POINTS

PRAYER STRATEGY

Which strategy did God give you in prayer?

OTHER REFERENCE SCRIPTURES ABOUT MANAGE WHAT YOU HAVE:

_____
_____
_____
_____
_____

UNLEASHED TO LEAD (LEADERSHIP APPLICATION)

As a leader, you have a responsibility to be as productive as you can be. There is a feast made for kings that is waiting for you to partake. You can't afford to be stubborn. You can't even afford to be fearful. If you're not prosperous, it will be your fault. "Eat the fruit of the land" is translated as follows: 1) the best crops in the land will be yours (CEV); 2) you'll feast like kings (MSG); 3) you will get the good things from this land (ERV); 4) you will eat the good things the land produces; 5) you will have plenty to eat (NLT). What will you do to get your harvest and live in prosperity?

_____
_____
_____
_____
_____
_____
_____
_____
_____
_____
_____
_____
_____

DEMONSTRATE: Every seed you have sown is designed to produce a harvest. Complete this chart below to assess your seedtime and harvest lifestyle:

Seedtime (describe seeds you've sown)	Harvest (describe fruit you've manifest)	Harvest (describe fruit you expect to manifest)

IMPACT

How does today impact your prosperity?

_____

_____

_____

_____

_____

_____

_____

_____

_____

_____

QUOTE OF THE DAY

❝ God is about to increase you more financially than what you are expecting for. When He gets finished, you will have enough to take care of you, your children, and somebody else. You will be blessed and you will become a blessing in Jesus's name. Amen. ❞

-Apostle Jonathan Ferguson

Apostle Jonathan Ferguson, Wealth Zones: How to Locate Your Economic Zip Code, (Ferguson Global, 2014), 39.

Day 17: GIVE, GIVE, GIVE

Luke 6:38 (AMPC) "Give, and [gifts] will be given to you; good measure, pressed down, shaken together, and running over, will they pour into [the pouch formed by] the bosom [of your robe and used as a bag]. For with the measure you deal out [with the measure you use when you confer benefits on others], it will be measured back to you."

ABOUT DAY 17

This is one of my favorite aspects of prosperity. I love to give, give, give. But some of us lack, lack, lack because our fists are closed so tightly. I believe our fists are closed because we don't understand the principle in the scripture above. It's simple though. Give sparingly, reap sparingly. Give bountifully, reap bountifully. Are you ready for the running over blessings? Then give, give, give.

TAKE ACTION

Describe how you tithe (how much, how often, to whom?).

Describe how you sow (how much, how often, to whom?).

Describe how you make charitable donations (how much, how often, to whom?).

AFFIRMATION

I will give in good measure and I expect to be blessed 30, 60, 100-fold, plus. I am a cheerful giver.

THOUGHTS FOR YOUR JOURNAL

Is your money at the level you desire it to be?
How much do you give/donate monthly?
In which areas do you give (i.e., tithes, sowing, donations)?

DAY 17 PRAYER POINTS

Father God, I want to be the greatest tither in my church; I want to have the largest giving charitable organization, and I want to help the most people. Thank you for my gift of giving. Thank you that because of my wealth my entire family will be set free from poverty because I give, give, give.

YOUR DAY 17 PRAYER POINTS

PRAYER STRATEGY

Which strategy did God give you in prayer?

OTHER REFERENCE SCRIPTURES ABOUT GIVE, GIVE, GIVE:

_____
_____
_____
_____
_____

UNLEASHED TO LEAD (LEADERSHIP APPLICATION)

One of the most important mindsets of a leader is a servant or giving mindset. Describe how you have a giving mentality.

_____
_____
_____
_____
_____
_____
_____
_____
_____
_____
_____
_____
_____
_____
_____
_____
_____

DEMONSTRATE

A Few Ways to Give	Commitment	Dates
1. Sow		
2. Tithe		
3. Donate	Salt and Light Evangelistic Association, Incorporated (501c3) charitable organization focused on historically disadvantaged men and boys (i.e., homeless, incarcerated, students).	
4. Offering		
5. Give to Family & Friends		
6. Serving		

IMPACT

How does today impact your prosperity?

_____
_____
_____
_____
_____
_____
_____
_____
_____
_____

QUOTE OF THE DAY

“ The truth of the matter is that the enemy desires to use every means possible in order to either convince people that God wants Christians broke, or to even discredit the integrity of Christian leaders in the area of money. ”

-Apostle Jonathan Ferguson

Apostle Jonathan Ferguson, Wealth Zones: How to Locate Your Economic Zip Code, (Ferguson Global, 2014), 11.

Day 18: OPEN UP YOUR HANDS

Proverbs 28:19-20 (NIV) "Those who work their land will have abundant food, but those who chase fantasies will have their fill of poverty. A faithful person will be richly blessed, but one eager to get rich will not go unpunished."

ABOUT DAY 18

Isn't this another powerful scripture? This Word helped me with my dilemma so much. How much work do I put in? Leaders, we have to put in work and work diligently and we will have the abundance and prosperity that is ours by birthright anyway. Curses manifest when we are disobedient. We're chasing fantasies when we don't work our land. For a kingdom leader to work, she must serve not only her land but serve the kingdom. To till or work is to labor or work as a servant. You are required to work what you own. You serve in your sphere of influence and you take care of what prospers you – your gifts, your talents, your leadership, your products, your services.

TAKE ACTION

Make short term and long term financial goals.

Set priorities for your savings each quarter.

Make a land, property, and real estate plan.

AFFIRMATION

I will faithfully work my land with steadfastness and prepare my hands to receive blessings and prosperity.

THOUGHTS FOR YOUR JOURNAL

How do you work your land (what you own, your gifts, talents real estate, possessions)?
Trace your mindset about money and prosperity.
Do you believe it is wrong to be rich and prosperous?
What are your current living circumstances and how will you improve them?

_____

_____

_____

_____

_____

_____

_____

_____

_____

_____

_____

_____

_____

_____

_____

_____

_____

_____

_____

_____

_____

_____

_____

_____

DAY 18 PRAYER POINTS

Father God, I want to demolish any scarcity, lack, and poverty mindsets that cause me to reject my prosperity. Reveal to me when I'm venturing into chasing fantasies and lead me back to You again. Prepare my heart and mind now for all the abundance, prosperity, and blessings that I'm claiming now in Jesus's name.

YOUR DAY 18 PRAYER POINTS

PRAYER STRATEGY

Which strategy did God give you in prayer?

OTHER REFERENCE SCRIPTURES ABOUT OPEN YOUR HANDS:

_____
_____
_____
_____
_____

UNLEASHED TO LEAD (LEADERSHIP APPLICATION)

As a leader, much is given to you and much is required. You are kingdom. You represent the kingdom. You're an ambassador for the kingdom. When the world sees you, they should see what God does for those in His kingdom. What are the kingdom provisions God has made for you? Which provisions do you want Him to make?

_____
_____
_____
_____
_____
_____
_____
_____
_____
_____
_____
_____
_____
_____
_____
_____
_____

DEMONSTRATE: You are a lender, not a borrower.

Land, Property and Real Estate Plan (Work the Land You Own)			
Goal	Actions/Strategy/ Intervention	Amount to Be Saved Monthly	Timeline
1. First home			
2. Second home			
3. Commercial Property			
4. Beach front/ Retirement home			
5. Rental Property			
6. Home for Child(ren)			

EXTENDING THE STRATEGY: FINANCIAL GOALS & PRIORITIES

Short term financial goals:

_____

_____

_____

Long term financial goals:

_____

_____

_____

Savings priorities:

_____

_____

_____

IMPACT

How does today impact your prosperity?

_____

_____

_____

_____

_____

_____

_____

_____

_____

_____

_____

_____

_____

_____

QUOTE OF THE DAY

" It is true that God wants us wealthy, but whether we desire the capacity to receive that wealth is totally up to us. **"**

-Apostle Jonathan Ferguson

Apostle Jonathan Ferguson, Wealth Zones: How to Locate Your Economic Zip Code, (Ferguson Global, 2014), 12.

Day 19: PRODUCE YOUR WEALTH

Deuteronomy 8:18 (AMPC) "But you shall [earnestly] remember the Lord your God, for it is He Who gives you power to get wealth, that He may establish His covenant which He swore to your fathers, as it is this day."

ABOUT DAY 19

One of the most important things to God is that He gets our worship, praise, faith, and ALL the glory. That is why the love of money is the root of all evil. God wants us to remember Him and give Him all the credit when He blesses us with our prosperity. He reminds us here again that in all our dominating as leaders, He is the One who gave us the power to get the wealth we're walking into. As smart and savvy as we may be as leaders, remember the Lord your God. He did this!

TAKE ACTION

Make a monthly budget with allocations for each category.

Use the envelope system.

Reduce spending on certain items (i.e. coffee, eating out).

AFFIRMATION

I claim that I will earn/save at least _____ in Jesus's name. Satan take your hand off my money. Ministering spirits, cause my money to come to me now.

THOUGHTS FOR YOUR JOURNAL

In what ways has the power within you worked to help you get wealth?

If you haven't produced wealth yet, why not?

Trace any mistakes you've made in spending and/or saving money. How will you correct your mistakes?

How can you continue to move forward in your purpose in spite of your mistakes?

DAY 19 PRAYER POINTS

Father God, I want to remain humble and always give You all the glory. I bind the spirit of mammon in Jesus's name. I bind any pride in me now. I thank You for the power that is already in me to produce the wealth I desire for kingdom building and to answer my needs.

YOUR DAY 19 PRAYER POINTS

PRAYER STRATEGY

Which strategy did God give you in prayer?

OTHER REFERENCE SCRIPTURES ABOUT PRODUCE YOUR WEALTH:

_____
_____
_____
_____
_____

UNLEASHED TO LEAD (LEADERSHIP APPLICATION)

As a leader, you have to be savvy in budgeting and managing larger and larger sums of money. Complete the following activity, The 30 Day Envelope Budget. Determine how many categories you have in your budget and that will be the same number of envelopes you will need. Put money for each category of your budget in envelopes and do not spend over the amount in each category and do not borrow from other envelopes (i.e., tithes, seed, gifts/donations, education, groceries, restaurants, gas, health, hair care, car, personal, etc.).

_____
_____
_____
_____
_____
_____
_____
_____
_____
_____
_____
_____

DEMONSTRATE: Tracking Your Spending

Where is Your $	Did you spend? Yes? Check the circle when you spend.						
	M	T	W	TH	F	S	S
Coffee/Soda	○	○	○	○	○	○	○
Eating Out	○	○	○	○	○	○	○
Snacks	○	○	○	○	○	○	○
Nails/Toes	○	○	○	○	○	○	○
Clothing	○	○	○	○	○	○	○
Shoes	○	○	○	○	○	○	○
Entertainment	○	○	○	○	○	○	○

IMPACT

How does today impact your prosperity?

_____
_____
_____
_____
_____
_____
_____
_____
_____

QUOTE OF THE DAY

" First. Fix in your mind the exact amount of money you desire. It is not sufficient merely to say 'I want plenty of money.' Be definite as to the amount. Second. Determine exactly what you intend to give in return for the money you desire. There is no such thing as something for nothing. Third. Establish a definite date when you intend to possess the money you desire. Fourth. Create a definite plan for carrying out your desire and begin at once, whether you are ready or not, to put this plan into action. Fifth. Write out a clear, concise statement of the amount of money you intend to acquire, name the time limit for its acquisition, state what you intend to give in return for the money, and describe clearly the plan through which you intend to accumulate it. Sixth. Read your written statement aloud, twice daily, once just before retiring at night, and once after arising in the morning. As you read, see and feel and believe yourself already in possession of the money. "

- Napoleon Hill

Napoleon Hill, Think and Grow Rich, (1937), 18.

Day 20: CREATE MULTIPLE STREAMS

Ecclesiastes 11:2 (NIV) "Invest in seven ventures, yes, in eight; you do not know what disaster may come upon the land."

ABOUT DAY 20

We say we have no money but we only work one job or have one stream of income. The Word says invest in seven ventures. I'm not advocating that you should have all these different jobs and business ventures that don't connect to your purpose. If you have a calling or mandate or wealth building like me, let me know so we can work together. God has shown me how to align my leadership business ventures: mindset, worth, and wealth. All my products and services will align with those concepts. Are you relying on and giving everything you have to one venture? You never know what may happen so invest in a few ventures.

TAKE ACTION

Research business ventures you can invest in to augment your income.

Map out where you're going in your finances and your leadership.

Pay attention to triggers that get you off focus.

AFFIRMATION

I will seek God about which ventures to give to and invest in and I will yield prosperous returns on all my investments because His hands are on me.

THOUGHTS FOR YOUR JOURNAL

How many streams of income do you have now? How much
do you make in each?
How much are your bills each month?
What are three statements you can write and then read
when you lose focus that will help you get refocused?
What is important about money to you?

DAY 20 PRAYER POINTS

Father God, I don't want to invest in another program or venture or business in which You didn't approve. I want You to be my Chief Financial Officer from now on. I want You to be my Investment Banker. Help me prepare for the times of wealth ahead in Jesus's name. Show me where you want me to invest.

YOUR DAY 20 PRAYER POINTS

PRAYER STRATEGY

Which strategy did God give you in prayer?

OTHER REFERENCE SCRIPTURES ABOUT PRODUCE YOUR WEALTH:

_____
_____
_____
_____
_____

UNLEASHED TO LEAD (LEADERSHIP APPLICATION)

As a leader, you need to be organized. Do you know where your money is? Organize all your bills in folders and create a filing system for all your financial documentation and other important documents (i.e., your will, SSN and card, copy of your license, mortgage statement, banks statements, in a locked file).

_____
_____
_____
_____
_____
_____
_____
_____
_____
_____
_____

IMPACT

How does today impact your prosperity?

_____

_____

_____

_____

_____

_____

_____

_____

_____

_____

_____

QUOTE OF THE DAY

" The problem is not our income, it's what we spend." **"**

-David Bach

EXTENDING THE STRATEGY: INVESTMENT ACCOUNTS

Are you ready to open an investment account? Research and decide on the entity you will use to invest. Start small and safe and pray for wisdom about how much you invest monthly.

David Bach, Smart Women Finish Rich: 9 Steps to Achieving Financial Security and Funding Your Dreams (Broadway Books, 1999), 21.

Day 21: PUT YOUR MONEY TO WORK

Luke 19:26 "He replied, "I tell you that to everyone who has, more will be given, but as for the one who has nothing, even what they have will be taken away."

ABOUT DAY 21

Make sure you go back and read Luke 19:11-26. The master in the parable took the money from the man who didn't multiply the money the master gave him. The master took it and gave it to a man who already made ten more than the master gave him. Everyone said "But Master he already has ten." Sometimes we look at other women leaders who are prospering greatly and it seems as if Jesus is giving them more than he gave us. But are they putting their money to work and multiplying what Jesus gave them and we're not?

TAKE ACTION

Make yourself an expert in your area of leadership.

Stand out in the area of your finances (i.e., tithing, sowing, saving, spending, investing).

Be a model and example in your leadership and finances.

AFFIRMATION

I will take what You have given me Jesus and multiply it. I will be a good steward over what you gave me. I give freely but I gain even more. You will give me more because I am faithful now.

THOUGHTS FOR YOUR JOURNAL

What do you have right now?
How are you taking what you have and multiplying it?
If you could do anything in the world, what would you do?
If you could help other women do anything, what would it be?

DAY 21 PRAYER POINTS

Father God, I want to thank You that I have money. I thank You for trusting me with more. I thank You for prospering me. I thank You for revealing to me where to invest, what to do and how to do it so I can put my money to work. I thank You for teaching me how to multiply what You gave me.

YOUR DAY 21 PRAYER POINTS

PRAYER STRATEGY

Which strategy did God give you in prayer?

_____
_____
_____
_____
_____

UNLEASHED TO LEAD (LEADERSHIP APPLICATION)

As a leader, you have to be able to distinguish between what are wants or needs, and what is kingdom. Make 3 columns and write down every financial want, need, and kingdom requirement. Prioritize how you will meet these wants, needs and requirement. Brainstorm here.

_____
_____
_____
_____
_____
_____
_____
_____
_____
_____
_____
_____
_____
_____
_____
_____

Wants	Needs	Kingdom Priorities

EXTENDING THE STRATEGY: SAVINGS
Open a savings account for a specific goal
(e.g., house, business, 9-12-month emergency fund).

LEADERSHIP PROFILE:

What changes have you seen in yourself?	What mindset changes have you seen?	How do you react differently to different situations?

IMPACT

How does today impact your prosperity?

_____
_____
_____
_____
_____
_____
_____
_____
_____

QUOTE OF THE DAY

MANIFESTATION

What has manifested in your life in the area of peace in your purpose?	What has manifested in your life in the area of progress in your purpose?	What has manifested in your life in the area of prosperity in your purpose?

WEEK THREE REVIEW:

Today, pray and seek God for how to accept His prosperity for your life. Write the steps God gives you for how to produce wealth. Make sure you are in alignment with His purpose for you. Receive His prosperity for you.

David Bach, Smart Women Finish Rich: 9 Steps to Achieving Financial Security and Funding Your Dreams (Broadway Books, 1999), 17.

YOU HAVE
Peace
YOU'RE MAKING
Progress
YOU'RE ACHIEVING YOUR
Prosperity

Made in United States
Orlando, FL
17 December 2021

11946175R00070